INTRODUCTION

Mr. Chairman and distinguished members of the committee, I am honored to join you today. I appreciate the opportunity to testify about the posture of United States strategic forces, my assessment of the President's Fiscal Year 16 (FY16) Budget, and how United States Strategic Command (USSTRATCOM) is confronting today's complex global security environment. I am also pleased to be here with General Paul Selva, Commander of United States Transportation Command; and Admiral Mike Rogers, Commander of United States Cyber Command. I thank Congress and this committee for your support to our Nation's defense.

I am pleased to report that USSTRATCOM remains capable and ready to meet our assigned missions and that the Nation's strategic nuclear deterrent force remains safe, secure, and effective. USSTRATCOM is focused on deterring strategic attack and providing assurance to our allies while providing combat support to our Joint Military Forces and other Combatant Commands across the spectrum of their operations to support national security and strategic stability. While executing our global responsibilities, we made progress toward forging enduring partnerships with agencies and organizations across the U.S. government, commercial industry, and Allied nations. We took part in a number of vigorous exercises and thought-provoking wargames, and we participated in and conducted penetrating reviews of our nuclear enterprise.

Having traveled extensively to meet first-hand the men and women who carry out and support our strategic missions, I can personally attest to the talent, dedication and professionalism of the military and civilian personnel conducting these missions. Without doubt, our success to date is largely due to those who dedicate themselves to national security in spite of uncertainty and resource challenges. I want to publicly acknowledge their service and devotion to duty and country.

Today's complex and dangerous global security environment demands that we properly sustain and modernize our strategic capabilities. The President's FY16 Budget strikes a responsible balance between national priorities and fiscal realities, and begins to reduce some of the risk we have accumulated because of deferred maintenance and sustainment as we pursue modernization. This budget supports my mission requirements, but I remain concerned that if we do not receive relief from the Budget Control Act, we will experience significant risk in providing the U.S. with the strategic capabilities it needs. We cannot as a Nation afford to underfund these vital missions.

GLOBAL SECURITY ENVIRONMENT

The world today remains complex, dynamic, and uncertain. The military capabilities of nation states and non-state actors are improving across all domains. Nations around the world continue to execute long-term military modernization programs, including capabilities that pose an existential threat to the United States. Additionally, non-state actors show increasing ability to strategically impact worldwide stability and the security of the U.S. and our key allies. Nuclear weapon ambitions and nuclear, chemical and biological technologies proliferation continue, increasing the risk that others will resort to Weapons of Mass Destruction (WMD) coercion in regional crises or WMD use in future conflicts.

Russia took a number of troubling actions in 2014: intrusions into Ukraine, to include the attempted annexation of Crimea, violation of the Intermediate-range Nuclear Forces Treaty, long-range bomber flights penetrating U.S. and Allied defensive zones, and strategic force exercises conducted in the midst of the Ukraine crisis. Russia has pursued more than a decade of investments and modernization across their strategic nuclear forces. Russia also has significant cyber capability, as evidenced by events in Estonia, Georgia and Ukraine. Russia has also publicly stated they are developing non-nuclear precision-strike, cyber and counter-space capabilities, and Russian leaders openly maintain that they possess anti-satellite weapons and conduct anti-satellite research.

China is increasingly using low intensity coercion to advance its near abroad agenda with respect to sovereignty disputes. Combined with an overall lack of military transparency, its investment in capabilities such as counterspace technologies raises questions about China's global aspirations. According to the International Monetary Fund, China's gross purchasing power recently exceeded our own for the first time. China is using that wealth to modernize its strategic forces by enhancing existing silo-based ICBMs, conducting flight tests of a new mobile missile, and developing a follow-on mobile system capable of carrying multiple warheads. Strategic modernization extends to naval capabilities as China continues testing and integration of new ballistic missile submarines, their first sea-based strategic nuclear deterrent. China is also developing multi-dimensional space capabilities supporting their access-denial campaign. With more than 60 nations operating satellites in space, China needs to be more forthcoming about missile tests that appear to be more focused on the development of destructive space weapons. China has also made headlines associated with exploitation of computer networks.

Other states such as North Korea, Iran, and Pakistan are working to advance their strategic capabilities. North Korea in particular continues work to advance their nuclear ambitions, to include conducting multiple nuclear tests and claiming a miniaturized warhead capable of delivery by ballistic missile. At the same time, North Korea continues to advance its ballistic missile capability, including the development of a new road-mobile ballistic missile and a submarine-launched ballistic missile; and develop its offensive cyber capabilities.

We remain concerned about Iran's nuclear activities and as a government remain dedicated to preventing them from acquiring a nuclear weapon. I remain hopeful that the P5-plus-1 negotiations will have the desired effect. Like North Korea, there are also public examples of Iran's cyber activities and capabilities.

Ungoverned or ineffectively governed regions remain incubators for those who seek to attack targets in—and the values of—democratic societies across the globe. Terrorist threats continue to morph in both substance and style, and Violent Extremist Organizations (VEOs) recruit and operate freely across political and social boundaries. While natural biological threats such as Ebola challenge our capacity to contain and control them, WMD in the hands of unrestrained VEOs could prove catastrophic. Such a scenario highlights the importance of our countering WMD and our non-proliferation efforts. Finally, the Assad regime continues to engage in low-level tactical use of toxic industrial chemicals as weapons in Syria, while failing to fully address the omissions and discrepancies in its chemical weapons declaration to the Organization for the Prohibition of Chemical Weapons.

Space systems continue to enable a wide range of services, providing vital national, military, civil, scientific, and economic benefits to the global community. As the number of space-faring nations and commercial enterprises continue to grow, the space domain is becoming increasingly congested, contested, and competitive. Given the counter space initiatives by Russia, China, and others, we must continue to reinforce the peaceful use of space while ensuring continued space operations through partnerships and resiliency.

Our dependence on cyberspace and the electromagnetic spectrum (EMS) creates risk. The worldwide cyber threat continues to grow, with state and non-state actors targeting U.S. networks on a daily basis. Today, a small number of cyber actors have the potential to create large-scale damage. While most cyber threats can be characterized as criminal in nature, wide-ranging intrusions and attacks have threatened critical infrastructure and impacted commercial enterprise. Likewise, our use of the EMS has become so commonplace that we largely take spectrum access for granted. The global proliferation of once-restricted technologies allows adversaries and potential adversaries to directly challenge our freedom of maneuver and our ability to operate in the EMS and in cyberspace.

Finally, uncertainty continues to manifest in other ways such as social unrest and turmoil, regional competition for scarce resources and economic opportunities, naturally occurring phenomena such as climate change and disease, and rapid proliferation of empowering technologies. Additionally, the concept of mating advanced weapon systems with commonplace items—such as surface-to-surface cruise missiles disguised as shipping containers—blurs the line between military and civilian environments and complicates our deterrence calculus.

USSTRATCOM IN THE 21ST CENTURY

USSTRATCOM counters these diverse and complex threats through the execution of its fundamental mission: **to deter and detect strategic attacks against the U.S. and our allies, and to defeat those attacks if deterrence fails**. USSTRATCOM is assigned nine distinct responsibilities: **Strategic Deterrence**; **Space Operations**; **Cyberspace Operations**; **Global Strike**; **Joint Electronic Warfare**; **Missile Defense**; **Intelligence, Surveillance and Reconnaissance**; **Countering Weapons of Mass Destruction**; and **Analysis and Targeting**. These diverse assignments are strategic in nature, global in scope, and intertwined with Joint Force capabilities, the interagency and the whole of government. **Each mission supports or is interconnected with the others, and their combined capabilities create the conditions for strategic deterrence against a variety of threats.**

Deterrence is a fundamentally human endeavor, firmly rooted in psychology and social behavior. At the most basic level, deterrence is achieved through one of two mechanisms. The first is an aggressor's recognition that unacceptable costs may be imposed for taking an action and recognition that forgoing said action may avoid these costs. The second is an aggressor's belief that the contemplated action will not produce its perceived benefit, or that not acting will produce a greater perceived benefit. These elements combine to convince potential adversaries that they will not succeed in an attack, and even if they try, the costs will far outweigh the benefits and thus restraint is the preferred choice. These fundamental elements of deterrence are well understood, and are supported by USSTRATCOM's capabilities.

Strategic deterrence in the 21st century is far more than just nuclear, although our nuclear deterrent remains the ultimate guarantor of our security. It includes a robust intelligence apparatus; space, cyber, conventional, and missile defense capabilities; and comprehensive plans that link organizations and knit their capabilities together in a coherent way. America's nuclear deterrent—a synthesis of dedicated sensors, assured command and control, the triad of delivery systems, nuclear weapons, enabling infrastructure, trained ready people, and treaties and non-proliferation activities—remains foundational to our national security and has been a constant thread in the geopolitical fabric of an uncertain world. The likelihood of major conflict with other nuclear powers is remote today, and the ultimate U.S. goal remains the achievement of a world without nuclear weapons. Until that day comes, the U.S. requires a safe, secure and effective nuclear deterrent force, even as it continues to reduce its nuclear stockpile and the number of deployed nuclear warheads. As stated in the 2014 Quadrennial Defense Review (QDR), our nuclear deterrent capabilities "…deter nuclear attack on the United States, as well as on our allies and partners" and communicate "…to potential nuclear-armed adversaries that they cannot escalate their way out of failed conventional aggression."

USSTRATCOM efforts are guided by my six overarching priorities. **My number one priority is to deter strategic attack.** Strategic attacks can occur through a variety of mechanisms in any domain and are defined by their scope and their decisive negative outcomes for the Nation. They may impact many people or systems, affect large physical areas, act across great distances, persist over long periods of time, disrupt economic or social structures, or change the status quo in a fundamental way. We must continue our efforts to deter strategic threats to global stability.

Second, we will provide the Nation with a safe, secure and effective nuclear deterrent force. Foundational documents such as the 2010 Nuclear Posture Review, the 2013 Report on Nuclear Weapons Employment Strategy, and the 2014 QDR have consistently repeated this mandate. It is my responsibility to provide our Nation with a viable and credible nuclear deterrent force as long as nuclear weapons exist.

Third, we will build enduring relationships with partner organizations to confront the broad range of global challenges. We aim to work seamlessly across the federal government, commercial sector, and with partners and Allies to apply the breadth of USSTRATCOM capabilities toward a synchronized pursuit of national objectives. Robust interaction occurs at all levels in our organization and includes operations, exercises and wargames with other Combatant Commands and Allies.

Fourth, we will continue to address challenges in space. Space capabilities remain foundational to our way of life, yet are increasingly vulnerable to hostile actions. Robust space domain awareness remains central to our ability to maintain an advantage in space.

Fifth, we must continue to build cyberspace capability and capacity. Cyberspace supports operations extensively in all of my mission areas and has become a critical facet of national power. We must continue to develop a robust cyber mission force with the authorities, skills, and resources to protect against a maturing set of cyber threats.

Finally, geopolitical and fiscal realities demand that we anticipate change and confront uncertainty with agility and innovation. Sound decision-making requires thorough analysis to prioritize our activities along with flexible, agile, adaptable thinking and systems. I fully support the Defense Innovation Initiative and the associated Advanced Capability and Deterrence Panel. These efforts will help us identify new operational concepts, develop cutting edge technology, and enable a continuing evolution of ideas on how to deter current and potential adversaries.

MISSION AREA CAPABILITIES & REQUIREMENTS

Even the best analysis will never be error free, so we must maintain adequate readiness to confront uncertainty. Prioritizing resources to meet our requirements requires a thoughtful assessment of national priorities in the context of fiscal realities. The President's FY16 Budget supports my mission requirements, but there is no margin to absorb risk. Any cuts to that budget—including those imposed by sequestration—will hamper our ability to sustain and modernize our military forces, and will add significant risk to our strategic capabilities now and in the future.

Nuclear Deterrent Forces

In the wake of a series of events involving the Nation's nuclear forces and their leadership, Secretary Hagel directed an internal and external review of the entire Department of Defense (DOD) nuclear enterprise. The reviews concluded that while our nuclear forces are currently meeting the demands of the mission, we needed to make significant changes to ensure the future safety, security, and effectiveness of the force. I fully support planned investments in the nuclear enterprise that will improve and sustain current equipment in response to these reviews.

Our nuclear deterrent is the ultimate insurance against a nuclear attack on the United States. We must commit to investments that will allow us to maintain this insurance in a safe and secure way for as long as nuclear weapons exist, or risk degrading the deterrent and stabilizing effect of a credible and capable nuclear force. Today we spend less than 3 percent of the DOD budget on nuclear capabilities. As stated by the Congressional Budget Office, recapitalization investments that are necessary to ensure safety and security will increase this number to "roughly 5 percent to 6 percent."

Sensors. Strategic missile warning remains one of our most important missions. Along with persistent and tailored intelligence capabilities, our Integrated Tactical Warning and Attack Assessment network of sensors and processing facilities provide timely, accurate, unambiguous, and continuous tactical early warning and allow us to select the most suitable course of action in rapidly developing situations. The Defense Support Program is nearing the end of its operational life, but the Space-Based Infrared System program is on track to provide continuous on-orbit capability. The survivable and endurable segments of these systems, along with Early Warning Radars and nuclear detonation detection elements, are in urgent need of continued simultaneous sustainment and modernization. We must continue to maintain legacy systems at ever-increasing risk to mission success. Prompt and sufficient recapitalization of these critical facilities and networks—to include electromagnetic pulse protection and survivable endurable communications with other nodes in the system—will be central to maintaining a credible deterrent. I fully support continued investment in this critical area.

Nuclear Command, Control and Communications (NC3). Assured and reliable NC3 is fundamental to the credibility of our nuclear deterrent. The aging NC3 systems continue to meet their intended purpose, but risk to mission success is increasing as key elements of the system age. The unpredictable challenges posed by today's complex security environment make it increasingly important to optimize our NC3 architecture while leveraging new technologies so that NC3 systems operate together as a core set of survivable and endurable capabilities that underpin a broader, national command and control system.

I appreciate Congress' direction last year to establish the Council on Oversight of the National Leadership Command, Control and Communications System (CONLC3S). The CONLC3S has proven effective in bringing NC3 stakeholders together to synchronize and prioritize NC3 modernization efforts, and then articulate those priorities to Congress. Specific programs include the Family of Beyond-line-of-sight Terminals, Presidential National Voice Conferencing, the Multi-Role Tactical Common Data Link, Phoenix Air-to-Ground Communications Network, the E-4B Low Frequency Transmit System, B-2 Common Very Low Frequency Receiver, and the E-6B service life extension and Airborne Launch Control System replacement programs.

The USSTRATCOM Command and Control (C2) Facility will support all our missions and will feature prominently in our future nuclear and national C2 architecture. The project is progressing well and will soon transition from exterior construction to interior fit-out. Timely, consistent, and stable funding is vital to keeping the project on-time and on-budget. I appreciate the steadfast support that Congress continues to provide for this effort.

Nuclear Triad. The policy of maintaining a nuclear triad of strategic nuclear delivery systems was most recently re-iterated in the 2014 QDR. Our Intercontinental Ballistic Missiles, Ballistic Missile Submarines, and nuclear capable heavy bombers each provide unique and complementary attributes that together underpin strategic deterrence—and each element is in need of continued investment.

Intercontinental Ballistic Missiles (ICBMs). Our ICBM force promotes deterrence and stability by fielding a responsive and resilient capability that significantly complicates the decision calculus of any potential adversary. Though first fielded in 1962, the Minuteman Weapon System is sustainable through 2030, with near-term investments in the Mk21 replacement fuze, ICBM Cryptographic Upgrade, Payload Transporter vehicle replacement, Transporter-Erector vehicle replacement, and UH-1N helicopter replacement programs to address age-related issues. The Air Force is initiating the Ground Based Strategic Deterrent program to begin recapitalizing the ICBM enterprise. USSTRATCOM fully supports an integrated weapon system recapitalization effort that synchronizes flight systems, ground systems, command and control, infrastructure, and support equipment development and deployment.

Ballistic Missile Submarines (SSBNs). Recapitalizing our sea-based strategic deterrent force is my top modernization priority. The Navy's SSBNs and Trident II D5 ballistic missiles constitute the Triad's most survivable leg. In 2014, the Ohio-class fleet completed the submarine force's 4000th strategic deterrent patrol. This stealthy and highly capable force is undergoing needed modernization to extend the life of the D5 missile and replace the Ohio-class SSBNs which begin to retire in 2027. No further extension is possible and maintaining operational availability is a concern. We must resource sustainment of the Ohio class SSBNs to maintain the required availability through the transition period to the Ohio Replacement Program (ORP) SSBN and until the last hull is decommissioned in 2040. Stable funding of the ORP, the life-of-ship reactor core, and supporting systems and infrastructure is critical to achieving a first deterrent patrol in 2031. In addition, we must continue our commitment to the United Kingdom to develop and field the Common Missile Compartment to ensure both nations' SSBNs achieve operational capability on schedule.

Heavy Bombers. Our dual-capable B-52 and B-2 bombers continue to provide significant conventional capabilities along with flexibility, visibility and a rapid hedge against technical challenges in other legs of the nuclear triad. Planned sustainment and modernization activities, to include associated NC3, will ensure a credible nuclear bomber capability through 2040. Looking forward, a new highly survivable penetrating bomber is required to credibly sustain our broad range of deterrence and strike options beyond the lifespan of today's platforms. Maintaining an effective air-delivered standoff capability is vital to meet our strategic and extended deterrence commitments and to effectively conduct global strike operations in anti-access and area-denial (A2AD) environments. The Long Range Stand-Off AoA completed earlier this year recommended a follow-on nuclear cruise missile to replace the aging Air Launched Cruise Missile (ALCM) with a capability designed for future adversary A2AD environments.

Weapons and Infrastructure. Nuclear weapons and their supporting infrastructure underpin our nuclear triad, with the average warhead today over 27 years old. Surveillance activities, Life Extension Programs (LEPs), and Stockpile Stewardship efforts are key to sustaining our nuclear arsenal by mitigating age-related effects and incorporating improved safety and security features without a return to nuclear testing.

As a member of the Nuclear Weapons Council (NWC) I work in close coordination with my DOD and Department of Energy counterparts to ensure we maintain a safe, secure and effective nuclear stockpile. Active and sustained execution of the NWC's long-term "3+2" strategy to deliver three ballistic missile and two air-delivered warheads is crucial to achieving this goal while addressing both near-term technical needs and future capability requirements. The W76-1 and B61-12 LEPs are on track and are necessary to maintain confidence in the reliability, safety and intrinsic security of our nuclear weapons. Early activities are underway supporting the cruise missile replacement by the late 2020s. The President's FY16 Budget supports this and ensures schedule alignment of the cruise missile delivery platform and its associated weapon.

Sustaining and modernizing the nuclear enterprise infrastructure—in physical and intellectual terms—is central to our long-term strategy. Continued material investment and maintaining an adequate pool of nuclear scientists and engineers is crucial to providing critical capabilities that meet our stockpile requirements.

Treaties. International agreements such as New Strategic Arms Reduction Treaty (New START), the Open Skies Treaty (OST), and the Intermediate-range Nuclear Forces (INF) Treaty contribute to strategic stability through transparency, confidence building, and verification. The State Department has primary responsibility for treaty administration, and USSTRATCOM remains closely involved in their execution.

New START's central limits and verification mechanisms reduce the likelihood of misperceptions and misunderstandings. Similarly, OST demonstrated its utility during the crisis in the Ukraine, where overflight missions allowed the 34 state parties to the treaty the opportunity to observe the situation on the ground, thereby supplementing other sources of information. In a similar vein, the INF Treaty promoted strategic stability by addressing capabilities of significant concern to our European Allies. While these agreements have served valuable roles in promoting strategic stability, treaty violations are a cause for concern.

The U.S. has a long-standing commitment to reducing the number of nuclear weapons consistent with national policy and geopolitical conditions. At the height of the Cold War, the U.S. had 31,000 nuclear warheads. When New START was ratified in February 2011, we had 1,800 deployed warheads. USSTRATCOM continues to work with the Office of the Secretary of Defense, the Joint Chiefs of Staff, and the Services to implement New START. To date, the U.S. and Russia have together conducted over 70 inspections and have exchanged more than 7,000 New START message notifications. In 2014, the U.S. finalized the New START force structure and completed de-MIRVing MM III ICBMs. Given the proper authority and funding, we are on track to achieve New START's limits of 1,550 deployed warheads, 700 deployed delivery systems, and 800 deployed and non-deployed delivery systems by February 2018.

Space Operations

The U.S. must maintain assured access to space. Our national space capabilities allow us to globally navigate, communicate, and observe natural and man-made events in areas where non-space sensors are either not available or not feasible. Space capabilities are also a key component of strategic deterrence. Our space sensors, command and control systems, and space situational awareness capabilities are critical to supporting both our deployed forces and our national decision making processes.

As articulated in the 2011 National Security Space Strategy, the space domain is contested, congested, and competitive. Our potential adversaries have signaled their ability to conduct hostile operations in space as an extension of the terrestrial battlefield, and consider these operations essential to deny U.S. forces the asymmetric advantages of space. To mitigate this trend, the U.S. continues to partner with responsible nations, international organizations and commercial firms to promote responsible, peaceful and safe use of space. We also strive to maximize the advantages provided by improved space capabilities while reducing vulnerabilities; and seek to prevent, deter, defeat and operate through attacks on our space capabilities.

Foundational to all of these efforts is sufficient Space Situational Awareness (SSA)—the information that allows us to understand what is on orbit, where it is and where it is going, and how it is being used. Our goal is to ensure space remains a safe domain for all legitimate users. Sharing SSA information and collaborating with other nations and commercial firms promotes safe and responsible space operations, reduces the potential for debris-producing collisions, builds international confidence in U.S. space systems, fosters U.S. space leadership, and improves our own SSA through knowledge of other owner/operator satellite positional data.

USSTRATCOM is committed to using the full capabilities of our overhead-persistent infrared systems for all relevant mission areas. We are actively partnering with the Intelligence Community to more effectively manage our intelligence requirements, share data, and ensure all of our assets are effectively working to support national priorities.

In accordance with U.S. law, USSTRATCOM has negotiated SSA Sharing Agreements and Arrangements with 46 commercial entities, two intergovernmental organizations (EUMETSAT and European Space Agency), and eight nations (France, Italy, Japan, Australia, Canada, South Korea, United Kingdom, and Germany) and is in the process of negotiating agreements with additional nations. Through these sharing agreements, USSTRATCOM assists partners with activities such as launch support; maneuver planning; support for on-orbit anomaly resolution, electromagnetic interference reporting and investigation; support for launch anomalies and de-commissioning activities; and on-orbit conjunction assessments.

At the nucleus of USSTRATCOM's approach to space security is both strategic and tactical mission assurance—ensuring Combatant Commanders have required access to space-based capabilities, achieved through freedom of action in space. USSTRATCOM's Joint Functional Component Command for Space (JFCC Space), located at Vandenberg Air Force Base in California, leads the efforts to ensure continuous and integrated space operations and routinely track tens of thousands of space objects in orbit around the Earth. This includes more than 1,100 active satellites owned and operated by approximately 60 nations and government consortia, plus hundreds of small commercial and academic satellites. In 2014, this allowed JFCC Space to issue more than 12,000 conjunction alerts, resulting in 121 collision avoidance maneuvers, to include several maneuvers by the International Space Station.

We must sustain judicious and stable investments to preserve the advantages we hold in this dynamic and increasingly complex environment. Examples include the Space Fence program which will greatly expand the capacity of the Space Surveillance Network, investments in modeling and simulation which will increase our understanding of the space environment and adversary capabilities, and funding for satellite communications that are resistant to interference. We must also continue to seek out innovative and cooperative solutions with Allies and partners to ensure the products and services we derive from operating in space remain available, even when threatened by natural events or the actions of a determined adversary. These include both active and passive protection measures for individual systems and constellations and a critical examination of the architectural path we will follow to ensure resilience and affordability in space.

Cyberspace Operations

This year marks the fifth anniversary of the activation of our assigned sub-unified command, US Cyber Command (USCYBERCOM) located at Ft. Meade, Maryland. USCYBERCOM seeks to impart an operational outlook and attitude to the running of the DOD's roughly seven million networked devices and 15,000 network enclaves—which represent a global system that operates at the speed of light beyond geographic and political boundaries.

Our primary focus for cyberspace operations within DOD is to increase capacity and capability. The Cyber Mission Force (CMF) construct addresses the significant challenges of recruiting, training, and retaining the people, facilities and equipment necessary to generate the workforce required for successful cyberspace operations. Our plans call for the creation of 133 cyber mission teams manned by more than 6,000 highly trained personnel by the end of FY16. To date, 61 of those teams are fielded and engaged in a variety of missions. The majority of these teams will support the combatant commands, with the remainder supporting national missions. It is imperative that we continue to pursue fulfilling our cyber capabilities. Budget stability is key to achieving this vision, as every training day we lose to fiscal constraints will cause further delays in fielding the CMF.

In order to posture the DOD to better defend against the growing number of threats, USSTRATCOM proposed the establishment of a Joint Force Headquarters – DOD Information Network (JFHQ-DODIN). The JFHQ-DODIN became operational in January 2015 and enables the Commander, USCYBERCOM to delegate authority for the operational and tactical level planning, execution, and oversight of DOD information network operations and defense to a subordinate unit. This arrangement ensures tactical mission success while allowing USCYBERCOM to remain focused on operational and strategic concerns.

Global Strike

USSTRATCOM's Joint Functional Component Command for Global Strike (JFCC-GS) operates from Offutt AFB, Nebraska with headquarters at Barksdale AFB, Louisiana. JFCC-GS provides a unique ability to command and control our global strike capabilities and build plans that rapidly integrate into theater operations. This includes integration of combat capability associated with kinetic and non-kinetic effects.

Conventional prompt strike (CPS) capability offers the opportunity to rapidly engage high-value targets without resorting to nuclear options. CPS can provide precision and responsiveness in A2AD environments while simultaneously minimizing unintended military, political, environmental, economic or cultural consequences. I support continuing research and development of capabilities that help fill the conventional strike gap with a discernible non-ballistic trajectory, maneuverability for over-flight avoidance, and payload delivery capability.

Effective strike solutions require dedicated analysis. USSTRATCOM's Joint Warfare and Analysis Center (JWAC) in Dahlgren, Virginia enhances our Strategic Deterrence and Global Strike missions by providing unique and valuable insight into selected adversary networks. JWAC's ability to solve complex challenges for our Nation's warfighters—using a combination of social and physical science techniques and engineering expertise—is invaluable to protecting the Nation and helping the Joint Force accomplish its missions.

Joint Electronic Warfare

America's prosperity and security relies on assured access to the electromagnetic spectrum (EMS) to achieve strategic advantage and enable the instruments of national power. The EMS reaches across geopolitical boundaries and warfighting domains, and is tightly integrated into the operation of critical infrastructures and the conduct of commerce, governance, and national security.

Joint Electromagnetic Spectrum Operations (JEMSO) underpin U.S. national objectives and enable the combat capability of the Joint Force by ensuring friendly access to the EMS while denying adversaries the same. USSTRATCOM is engaged in developing JEMSO policy and doctrine, and in addressing capability gaps across the DOD. Additionally, the USSTRATCOM JEMSO Office in conjunction with the Joint Electronic Warfare Center and Joint Electromagnetic Preparedness for Advanced Combat Center work closely with the combatant commands, Services and other Department agencies supporting the warfighter through advocacy, planning, and training.

Effective operations in the EMS will require development of an Electromagnetic Battle Management (EMBM) capability. The size and complexity of the EMS drives the requirement for the EMBM to be automated, interface at the machine level, and operate at near real-time speeds. This effort provides guidance for Service interoperability while retaining flexibility to meet Service-specific requirements. Future efforts will further refine and add context to the approved architectures.

Missile Defense

Effective missile defense is an essential element of the U.S. commitment to strengthen strategic and regional deterrence against states of concern. Today, 30 operational Ground Based Interceptors protect the U.S. against a limited ICBM attack from potential regional threats such as North Korea, but continued investment in three broad categories is required to improve our capabilities against growing threats: persistent and survivable engagement-quality tracking sensors, increased interceptor inventories with improved performance and reliability, and increased regional capability and capacity. These needs can be addressed by funding priority programs such as: Long-Range Discriminating Radar, a redesigned Exo-atmospheric Kill Vehicle (EKV), Aegis Ballistic Missile Defense and the Theater High-Altitude Area Defense follow-on, Overhead Persistent Infra-Red sensors, Upgraded Early Warning Radars, and Joint Tactical Ground Stations.

New technologies must be proven before we can count on them to contribute to our operational plans. I fully support the concept of "fly before you buy," and I was pleased by the Missile Defense Agency's successful test in June 2014 of the Capability Enhancement II EKV.

The European Phased Adaptive Approach (EPAA) contributes to the defense of the United States, our deployed forces in Europe, and our Allies. For example, the forward-based radar deployed in Turkey is capable of providing important early trajectory data on possible Iranian missile launches. EPAA Phase 1 was completed in 2011 and efforts are on track to fulfill Phase 2 and Phase 3 commitments in 2015 and 2018 respectively. Interoperability between NATO's Active Layered Theatre Ballistic Missile Defence system and the U.S. command and control network has been successfully demonstrated.

In December 2014, with the assistance of the Japanese Ministry of Defense, the DOD fielded a second AN/TPY-2 radar in Japan. The radar will augment the existing AN/TPY-2 radar and will enhance the ability to defend Japan, our forward deployed forces, and the U.S. homeland from North Korean ballistic missile threats.

The missile defense community—including USSTRATCOM's Joint Functional Component Command for Integrated Missile Defense (JFCC-IMD) located in Colorado Springs, Colorado—continued to refine its understanding of missile defense challenges from technical and resourcing perspectives. These include evaluating current and future sensor architectures to better integrate missile defense and situational awareness missions, studying potential CONUS interceptor sites, understanding current and future cruise and ballistic missile threats, improving

hit-to-kill assessment capabilities, and optimizing the location of missile defense assets.

Intelligence, Surveillance, & Reconnaissance (ISR)

The demand for ISR will always outpace our ability to fully satisfy all requirements. At

the same time, we are focused on the goal of increasing the effectiveness and persistence of our

ISR capabilities while reducing the "cost of doing business." Located at Joint Base Anacostia-

Bolling AFB, Washington, D.C., USSTRATCOM's Joint Functional Component Command for

ISR (JFCC-ISR) is working with our headquarters, the Joint Staff, the Services, the combatant

commands and the Intelligence Community to improve the management of the Department's

existing ISR capabilities given the high demands on these critical assets. I fully support this

maximizing the agile and effective use of the capabilities we have, while also enhancing allied

and partner contribution and cooperation. These efforts are designed to increase the persistence

of our ISR capabilities, reduce the risk of strategic surprise, and increase our ability to respond to

crises.

Countering Weapons of Mass Destruction (CWMD)

In June, the Secretary of Defense issued a new Defense Strategy for Countering WMD

which affirms that the pursuit of WMD and potential use by actors of concern pose a threat to

U.S. national security and peace and stability around the world. As DOD's global synchronizer

for CWMD planning efforts, USSTRATCOM supports this strategy by leveraging the expertise

resident in our Center for Countering Weapons of Mass Destruction (SCC-WMD), the Standing

Joint Force Headquarters for Elimination (SJFHQ-E), and our partners at the Defense Threat

Reduction Agency (DTRA)—all located at Ft. Belvoir, Virginia. Together, our organizations

conduct real-world and exercise CWMD activities with the other combatant commands to identify, prioritize, and mitigate WMD risks posed by proliferation of WMD technology and expertise to nation states and non-state actors.

USSTRATCOM contributed to the international effort to eliminate Syria's declared chemical weapons program in support of United States European and Central Commands. Additionally, SCC-WMD, SJFHQ-E, and DTRA personnel supported United States Africa Command's response to the 2014 Ebola outbreak in West Africa through the establishment of Regional Contingency Team – Ebola. The work conducted by this team—and the lessons learned along the way—will enable more effective responses to future natural or man-made biological threats.

To execute the DOD Strategy for CWMD, the CWMD community has identified a need for a comprehensive situational awareness capability that incorporates collaborative tools, continuously assesses the WMD threat, and provides a shared holistic awareness of the WMD environment. This capability would provide an enhanced awareness of emergent catastrophic-scale WMD threats that require continued collaboration across the interagency and partner nations to enable a proactive rather than reactive approach. We work closely with DTRA to develop this capability with input from our partners—such as the Intelligence Community and the Departments of State, Energy, Homeland Security and Justice—which will help us to clearly define operational information needs. Finally, there is an urgent need to update aging agent defeat weapons and develop modeling and simulation capabilities to assess collateral damage during WMD weapon attacks.

OUR PEOPLE

People remain our most precious resource and deserve our unequivocal commitment to their well-being. My travels throughout the past year visiting nuclear task forces, component commands, and USCYBERCOM confirmed my belief that we have an outstanding team in place across all of our mission areas. I am proud to serve alongside the men and women of USSTRATCOM and have the utmost respect for their professionalism, dedication to our missions, and sustained operational excellence.

We must continue to recruit and retain those who support the missions associated with strategic deterrence, from operators in the field to scientists in laboratories conducting surveillance and life extension work. We must directly support this unique workforce, but also ensure we support initiatives to keep them aware of our Nation's support for their important missions for the foreseeable future.

Whether they are underway on an SSBN, standing alert in a Launch Control Center, or supporting a mission from cyberspace to outer space, these great Americans will do all they can for their Nation, but are rightly concerned about their futures given continuing manpower reductions planned over the next several years. We are seeking the most efficient ways to achieve the Department's goals and are on track to do so, but cannot accommodate further cuts without a commensurate loss of organizational agility and responsiveness.

CONCLUSION

Achieving strategic deterrence in the 21st century requires an investment in strategic capabilities and a renewed, multi-generational commitment of intellectual capital. In today's uncertain times, I am honored to lead such a focused, innovative and professional group dedicated to delivering critical warfighting capabilities to the Nation. Your support, together with the hard work of the exceptional men and women of United States Strategic Command, will ensure that we remain ready, agile and effective in deterring strategic attack, assuring our Allies and partners, and addressing current and future threats.

www.ingramcontent.com/pod-product-compliance
Lightning Source LLC
Chambersburg PA
CBHW081432310526
45790CB00020B/3738